h·o·p·e·

FOUR KEYS TO A
BETTER QUALITY OF LIFE
FOR PARKINSON'S PEOPLE

~

HAL NEWSOM

Copies of HOPE are available from:

THE NORTHWEST PARKINSON'S FOUNDATION

400 Mercer Street #401

Seattle, WA 98109

Telephone (877) 980 7500

www.nwpf.org

Cost is $12.00 per copy. Send money order or check to

Northwest Parkinson's Foundation.

ISBN 0-9716841-0-3

This publication was underwritten by the author. It is made possible because of his
commitment to the broadening of education about Parkinson's Disease—especially for the
newly diagnosed who are just becoming acquainted with the disease. As a Board member
of the Northwest Parkinson's Foundation, Hal has asked that HOPE be distributed through
the Foundation, and that all proceeds go directly to the organization.

h·o·p·e·

ACKNOWLEDGEMENTS

A host of people helped make this book possible. A special thanks must go to Craig Howard of the Northwest Parkinson's Foundation. He was a master at editing and gave this endeavor guidance from conception to the final printing. Paul Cournoyer's skilled art direction breathed life into the project and made the content easy to read. He spent countless hours on the computer and at his design desk. Rod Olzendam of Leatherback Printing did a professional job of making sure the book was of the finest quality. Norm Hansen volunteered his production skills to prepare the digital files for printing. Peggy Newsom was a trusted grammarian and tireless proofreader. A "thank you" has to go to Dr. Phil Ballard and former Governor Booth Gardner who read the rough drafts and made helpful suggestions. And I would be remiss if I didn't mention the hundred or so people I've become acquainted with since being diagnosed. I have never been associated with a kinder, more compassionate group of individuals. They include those with the disease, caregivers, physicians, support group leaders, movement disorder specialists, foundation executives, and family members who are involved daily in helping loved ones find hope.

h·o·p·e·

FOREWORD

By Booth Gardner
Former Governor of the State of Washington

I've had Parkinson's Disease since 1993. I can say without hesitation that I wish Hal Newsom's book on HOPE had been available to me when I was first diagnosed. It's in a league of its own.

While there are many books available describing the parameters of the disease, this is the only book of which I am aware that humanizes the issue. It's written with a lot of heart, humor, and packed full of personal experiences which demonstrate that one can have a high quality of life while living with Parkinson's.

When you first hear the statement, "You have Parkinson's," it is a numbing blow. My first reaction was, "What is Parkinson's?" It took some research to learn about that tiny part of the brain that produces a chemical that sends signals to our nerve cells to control movement. It also came as a relief to learn that it causes no impairment in our ability to think or reason clearly.

Yet, the question remains: "What is my life going to be like?" The answer is: "Different."

I was traveling by air shortly after being diagnosed. Not being particularly fond of airplane meals in the economy section, I sought a snack during a layover in the terminal. While in line, a man three people ahead of me ordered a cup of soup. When he asked for crackers, he was referred to a side table. I noticed he had a tremor, and that he was having trouble getting the crackers out of the wrap. I had experienced similar frustrations. I asked the young woman in front of me if she would help him. She gave me a why don't you help him look. I explained that I thought he had Parkinson's and that I also had it. She shot me another look, then walked over, and said to him with a smile, "Let me help you."

You'll be amazed how much help is available. As Hal says in this book, "You'll do much better in coping with the disease if you acknowledge you may require help every now and then, both hands-on as well as moral support."

This wonderful book is full of thoughts on how to help the newly diagnosed reach a point where they can find a way to live each day to its fullest. I also recommend it as a guide and reminder for those of us who have been living with the disease for some time. And whether you're a person with Parkinson's, or a family member or friend, this is the place to start to find your H.O.P.E.

Booth Gardner

h·o·p·e·

THE ROLE OF THE NORTHWEST PARKINSON'S FOUNDATION

The Northwest Parkinson's Foundation was the brainchild of Bill Bell. His mother has Parkinson's and so do several of his relatives. Bill had a belief that if a Center for Parkinson's care could be developed it would be a means of improving the quality of life for Parkinson's People. He also felt the need for more information to the community about professional diagnosis and treatment. He envisioned a center with an on-staff physician trained specifically in the treatment of the disease, a physical therapist, an occupational therapist, a speech therapist, and a dietary specialist. In other words, a one-stop treatment center.

Bill enlisted Craig Howard to help him with the project. Soon these two men had the excitement of several Northwest leaders and a Board was formed. Financial help came quickly and it wasn't long before an association was developed with Evergreen Hospital in Kirkland, Washington. In the year 2000 the Booth Gardner Parkinson's Care Center was opened. The staff and the Foundation have brought new hope to thousands of Parkinson's People.

The Foundation has an on-going program of education to the general public, caregivers, those with the disease, and legislators. This book is only one of the many educational projects in which the Foundation is involved.

PREFACE

Hal Newsom retired from the advertising world at the age of 60, after spending 35 years writing television commercials, newspaper ads, and radio copy. He has always led an active physical life, filled with competitive sports and outdoor activities. At 66, he was diagnosed with Parkinson's Disease. Although slowed by Parkinson's, he has not let the disease diminish his zest for life. Today he hikes in the Washington mountains (not as high as before), downhill skis (except for moguls), jogs (at a snail's pace), and bikes the streets of Seattle (at no blazing speed). He shares his experiences and attitudes with the hope that they will help provide insight and encouragement to others who are identified in this book as Parkinson's People.

Hal defines Parkinson's People as individuals who have found a way to live each day to the fullest. He dislikes the term "Parkinson's patients" because it implies that they are awaiting care and guidance from someone else. Parkinson's People have the power to affect their quality of life. They may have had physical setbacks but they refuse to let these become unbearable burdens. They are vital, compassionate, mentally alert human beings who are changing the way society looks at Parkinson's Disease.

h·o·p·e·

h·o·p·e·

I have Parkinson's Disease. I don't know why. I suspect it could be related to one of several incidents that happened in my life. When I was 14, I was sledding one night and wound up with a concussion due to a pile-up at the bottom of the hill. When I was 16, I had a job in a paint factory and breathed toxic fumes throughout the summer. At a later stage in my life I drank well water that had a high manganese content. Did the knock-out blow cause damage to the dopamine producing brain cells? Did inhaling odors given off by the lead-laced paints render my substantia nigra less efficient in my senior years? Was the manganese the evil doer? I'm not sure. But how I got it is not as important as *what I am going to do about it now that I have it.*

SEARCHING FOR HOPE

The first few months of living with the idea that I had a disease that is defined as "progressive" was a serious adjustment. Shortly after being diagnosed, I attended a seminar given by a local hospital. One of the sessions was a display of Velcro clothing, long-handled shoe horns, oversized forks and spoons, walkers, and mechanical reachers for picking up items so you don't have to bend over. My emotional self wasn't ready to face the advanced stages of Parkinson's. I was simply looking for *hope*. I wanted to hear some words of encouragement.

h·o·p·e·

A few months later I attended a Saturday morning talk on the symptoms of Parkinson's given by a prominent neurologist. The good doctor spent nearly two hours covering restless leg syndrome, hallucinations, drenching sweats, intestinal pseudo-obstructions, respiratory ails, dyskinesia, sexual dysfunction, insomnia, pulmonary problems, and a host of other scary things. I was puzzled and confused. Once again I was looking for hope. I glanced around the room and saw some long faces. It was not an up-beat session for people who had recently been diagnosed.

These two experiences led me to examine what I meant by hope. A check of the <u>American Heritage Dictionary of the English Language</u> defined hope as: 1) A wish or desire supported by some confidence of its fulfillment; 2) A ground for expectation of trust; 3) That which is desired or anticipated; 4) That in which one places one's confidence; 5) Expectation; confidence.

I can't think of a more inspirational word. *Hope* can take away fear. It can brighten the outlook for tomorrow. It can bring laughter. It can inspire. It can clear away the clouds of uncertainty. Don't misunderstand—I'm not talking about "the cure" for Parkinson's. Recent research work shows encouraging signs. But a cure is still down the road. I <u>am</u> talking about coping with the disease in a manner that instills the *hope* necessary to live a better quality of life—particularly for the newly diagnosed Parkinson's Person.

h·o·p·e·

REMEMBER THOSE STARTLING WORDS

You can probably recall your exact emotions when the pronouncement came from the doctor, "You have Parkinson's." In a single sentence, what was your immediate reaction to your diagnosis?

I was: _____

_____

_____

I didn't include the word *hope* in my initial analysis and you probably didn't either. There was shock, disappointment and a little fear of the future. Truthfully, there was some hopelessness, rather than *hope*. My commitment to *hope* came after much reading, talking with Parkinson's friends and self-examination.

THE FOUR COMPONENTS OF HOPE

I believe there are four words that comprise the essentials of *hope*. They represent a mnemonic combination that helps make the components easy to remember:

1. HELP

    You'll be amazed how much help is available.

    Getting used to the idea you have Parkinson's can be a real adjustment. But you'll do a much better job of it if you acknowledge you may need help every now and then. It doesn't have to be hands-on physical help. It can be the moral support you have from a spouse, family, friends or fellow Parkinson's People. In addition, there is much information available which can be most helpful in understanding why your mind and body are acting the way they are. If you are accepting of the idea that you have Parkinson's, and can openly discuss your condition, help will open up to you in bountiful ways. Some personal experiences are covered in the Chapter on *help*.

2. OPTIMISM

If you have to have this disease, this is a good time to have it. There are new and more effective drugs, there are more specialists who can work with you with particular problems, there is more money going into research, and there is more encouragement that Parkinson's People can have a quality of life never possible before. When you remain up-beat and positive it improves your physical well-being as well as your joy of life. Some suggestions are offered later in this book.

3. PHYSICIAN

Your physician should be someone who specializes in movement disorders, specifically Parkinson's. He or she is one of your most important team members. This must be a person in whom you have complete confidence. There is no universal formula for treatment of Parkinson's. Every person is different. You and your physician will have to work out the medication strength and frequency of dosage. You have one big advantage today—there are lots of choices in your physician's medicine cabinet, and the odds are good that the right combination can be found quickly. How to get the most out of your physician and what your responsibilities are to him or her are discussed in the Physician section.

4. EXERCISE

You absolutely have to keep moving with this disease. You must be a disciplined exerciser. The old axiom, "Use it or lose it" is a guideline that must be respected. Daily stretching is important. Aerobic exercise will not only help your muscles and improve your body strength, it will help your heart stay healthy and give you a more positive outlook on the future. No one should undertake a vigorous program of exercise without a doctor's approval. The chapter on Exercise offers some hints on how to approach exercise—especially if you don't cotton to the idea.

h·o·p·e·

Help, Optimism, Physician and Exercise are the foundation of *hope*. Before we get into the details of how hope is working in my life, let me introduce you to four people who had to face the same problem: "How do I live with Parkinson's and enjoy a better quality of life?" You'll readily see that each had different adjustments, symptoms, and solutions. Can you identify with one or more of these Parkinson's People?

JACK

Jack is 63 years old. He's just retired. He was a machinist in a family-owned business where he was known as "the inventor," "the problem-solver" and "the Jack of all trades." He was good with his hands and had a quick mind. Over the last several years he had noticed it was more difficult twisting a screwdriver. His right hand didn't seem to have the strength to hold the screwdriver in place, and after a few turns he had to pause and massage his hand. He thought it might be arthritis.

SUE

When Sue turned 40 she thought she'd run in the local 10K Benefit For The Arts race. As she was lacing up her old Nike sneakers, she noticed her left shoe was worn quite badly. The right one showed little sign of wear. "Maybe that's why I've been tripping more frequently," was her thought. As a matter of fact, Sue had to keep her eyes on the pavement all the time to keep from catching her left foot on the slightest rise in the sidewalk. And when she was relaxing around the house, she would often trip on the dining room rug. "Pick up your feet," she would scold herself. Sue was vigorous, healthy and spirited, but she had a slight shuffle.

CARL

"You've got to do something about Dad," Jim told his mother. "What do you mean?" she replied. "Can't you see he's all bent over like an old man when he walks?" Jim explained. Carl's posture had slowly changed so that mother wasn't aware of his stooped shoulders and his head preceding his torso when he moved slowly through the house. But Jim had been away from home for six months. The physical changes were obvious to him. Carl wasn't the same old Dad.

BILL

Bill was sitting at his desk on a Monday morning. He had a very confrontational meeting coming up at 9:30. His lead salesman wasn't performing well and he had to find out why. Bill was nervous about how to handle the situation. He didn't want to be too firm or too wishy-washy either. He noticed his right hand was shaking a little. "Blasted nerves," he said. But then again, he'd noticed that he'd seen and felt his hand shake on numerous occasions. More numerous and with more   frequency than he was willing to admit. He rested his right hand on the desk, pressed down and this seemed to get the shake under control.

"YOU HAVE PARKINSON'S"

These people have one or more of the telltale signs of Parkinson's Disease—a scary term that conjures all sorts of negative feelings. Jack, Sue, Carl, and Bill each reacted differently when the doctor announced the shocking news. I remember that gray January day six years ago when I heard those chilling words. I didn't want to be destined to be a drooling fool, all hunched over and stumbling my way through advancing old age.

I have since learned there are tens of thousands of Parkinson's People who are involved in vibrant lives—playing golf, skiing, swimming, walking, running, playing bridge, attending theater, operas and symphonies, cooking, traveling, boating—even climbing mountains. _These are people who are not fighting the disease but who are successfully living with it._ They're not super heroes. They are ordinary people, with an un-ordinary health challenge.

Jack, Sue, Carl, and Bill are people I know who have had to face the new world of Parkinson's without too much encouragement from their doctors. So often the diagnosing physician is proficient in detecting the symptoms and formulating a valid conclusion, but it's been my observation that there are far too many incidents in which those much-needed words of encouragement are absent. It's probably understandable. The doctor can't control what your quality of life will be from diagnosis-day forward. That depends greatly upon your attitude and will power. Plus, it's difficult for the doctor to project how you will handle the pronouncement, "You have Parkinson's." Jack, Sue, Carl, and Bill each reacted to the news differently.

JACK, THE DISBELIEVER

Jack was stone-faced. He couldn't believe he had a disease called Parkinson's. His mind was as clear as a bell. It was only his hand. Not some brain malfunction. He had never heard of dopamine. And what's this about taking pills to get his nervous system to work better? Why, he'd never taken anything but an aspirin all his life–and that only about twice. He'd have to wait and see if the hand didn't improve. He felt silly having the doctor watch him walk down the hall and turn around. Maybe he moved a little slowly but that was because he was tired. He didn't have what the doctor called a tremor or the shakes. He put the prescription in his pocket with some reservation. Maybe he'd have it filled. Maybe he wouldn't. He'd wait and see. Maybe he ought to get a second opinion. If his condition didn't get any worse than it was, there was no need to make a big deal out of his problem. Maybe it would go away. He hoped it would go away.

SUE, THE PRO ACTIVIST

Sue was stunned. Her mind was filled with questions. How could a physically-fit 40 year old woman have an "old person's" sickness? How did she get it? What can she do about it? Is it fatal? How much dopamine has been lost? Will she be able to run? What about brain surgery? What's the best medication to take? How much should she take? Does it work? For how long? What stage of Parkinson's is she in? Who is the best specialist in the city? In the country? What kind of research is going on? Is there a cure? "I've got it. Now what am I going to do about it? The first thing I'm going to do is have a good cry."

CARL, THE ACCEPTOR

Carl took the news philosophically. If he had the dang disease, I guess he had it. The neurologist had recommended an MRI and that showed he didn't have a brain tumor or he wasn't suffering from a stroke. Parkinson's was better than brain damage. He wasn't too hot for taking medication for the rest of his life but the doctor said Sinemet would help his rigidity and slowness. He would follow his directions. After all, the doctor said the progression may be slow. He didn't like the diagnosis but what could he do about it? Most of all he hated telling his family about it. He didn't want to worry them.

BILL, THE ANGRY ONE

Bill was irritated. He was disturbed that the doctor gave him such shocking news so matter-of-factly. He could have been more compassionate. "After all, you are dealing with a person's life. My life. Why me?" He'd tried to take care of his health. Didn't smoke. Drank only occasionally. Exercised. He didn't like the idea of being a handicapped person. It's not how he pictured himself. It wasn't fair. What about the future? It would ruin his business career. He didn't want anyone to know except his wife. And what about his golf game? He didn't want to be seen as an old man with Parkinson's. "Oh, my gosh, look at that, the more I get upset, the more my hand shakes. I know what I'll do. I'll fight it and I'll lick it. I've always been able to succeed when I put my mind to it."

h·o·p·e·

WHAT HAPPENED TO YOU?

Can you identify with one of these people? Maybe there's a little of Sue and some of Bill in your initial diagnosis. Or you're a Jack with a leaning towards Carl. No matter how the doctor may try, there is no way to soften the blow of those thundering words, "You have Parkinson's." So often the words, "fear of the future," "anger," "hopelessness," "confusion," "loss" "disbelief," "growing old," "cheated," and "shame" describe the first emotions. Those are powerful negatives. It's certainly not a good news event. But it doesn't mean you have to get ready for 365 dark days of dismal doom every year. Or let the initial downer prevail for the rest of your life. An emotional adjustment is only natural. It's when and what you decide to do about your situation that will have such a positive bearing on your life. My fear of becoming a drooling old fool hasn't come to pass. As strange as it may seem, I've found *hope* in that and drawn strength from it. The truth is I've found *hope* in many different ways. But before we get to that, let's follow the progression of our four Parkinson's People.

JACK FACES PARKINSON'S

Denial is a reaction frequently experienced by newly diagnosed Parkinson's People. Jack is the perfect example of someone who will take several months or several years to face up to the reality that he is gradually getting slower, he doesn't feel up to par, his handwriting is getting more labored and smaller, he's bent over more and that blasted screwdriver still doesn't work. He will probably be a little short with his wife when she asks him to hurry and unlock the door while she's holding a bag of groceries. Communications with his wife and family will become increasingly more dificult. He is setting himself up for a bitter outlook on life, and he is feeling completely alone.

SUE FACES PARKINSON'S

Sue had her good cry. Then she set out to build a library of information about the disease. Initially she spent hours on the internet and was amazed how quickly her knowledge multiplied. She wrote to national Parkinson's associations for brochures on every conceivable subject—diet, speech, exercise, gait, support groups, and physical therapy. She figured, "If I've got the disease, then I should know all about it." She took her medication like clockwork–even kept a daily chart on the time of dosage and notes on her physical reactions. She called her doctor when the medication gave her nausea, and the dosage was changed. She felt better. But she was still aware every waking hour that her motor skills were not up to par. This was apparent in her running routine as she became slower. She just couldn't get her legs to turn over fast enough. She felt a loss that made her very emotional.

CARL FACES PARKINSON'S

Carl trusted his doctor. He was determined to live by the medication instructions as though they were the gospel. And so he did. He learned about "off" periods and "on" periods from his own personal experience. He didn't want to read too much about the disease and he didn't want to be around Parkinson's People in the advanced stages because that would depress him. For the same reason, he didn't want to join a support group. He knew Parkinson's was progressive, and he didn't want to be reminded of it. He discussed his condition with Lois, his wife, but it was a silent subject with his three children. He had his good days. And he had his bad days.

BILL FACES PARKINSON'S

Bill fought the diagnosis of Parkinson's every step of the way. He was concerned about his tremor and did everything he could to hide it. Frankly, he was embarrassed to be labeled a Parkinson's Person. He just couldn't be identified with the "handicapped" or "impaired". He took his daily doses of medication. He talked to his doctor quite frequently. It seemed like he couldn't find the right combination of drugs. But it was always difficult to reach his doctor when he needed her most. He thought, "Maybe I should change doctors." It was no fun having Parkinson's. He'd just have to fight a little harder. But he was always very fatigued.

DENIAL. A NATURAL TENDENCY

It's a common reaction to not want to believe what you've been told. A tremor can be justified as "just my nerves." Bill's attitude was that he would just have to fight a little harder. I have a friend who after three years from the initial diagnosis and changing physicians four times, finally has accepted that he "may have Parkinson's." He was an angry man, and unfortunately, his outbursts were not directed at the disease. He made his wife's life miserable and usually wound up shouting at his doctor.

You may not be able to achieve resolution until you've worked though your anger, recognized that you're entitled to grieve or experience the emotional pain of letting go. When you can say to yourself, "I have Parkinson's. I don't like the idea. But I'm not going to let it ruin my life," then you have more than likely worked through the stages of denial. That doesn't mean that you aren't going to have a little sadness every now and then. It does mean you are probably ready to accept the idea of *hope*.

It's important to remember that everyone you know will be affected as well—your spouse, your friends, your business associates, and your family members. They, too, may go through the phases of denial. They, too, may be experiencing disbelief, anger, grief, and final acceptance. They need encouragement, and your attitude has a direct affect on their *hope*. That's a tall order for someone who has recently been diagnosed, but it's all possible.

NO TWO PARKINSON'S PEOPLE ARE ALIKE

Parkinson's affects people in many different ways—physically and emotionally. No two people have the same symptoms. No two people have the same attitudes. Medication that works for Carl may not work for Bill. Sue doesn't have a tremor but she shuffles. Jack has hand dexterity problems. Carl is more bent over than Jack.

There is abundant information on the depletion of dopamine causing the disease and what the consequences may be—rigidity, slowness, tremor, and a host of other troublesome problems. There are research papers on new surgery techniques. There are newsletters all about medications. If all this is piled on a newly diagnosed Parkinson's Person, it can be overwhelming as well as discouraging. It's only natural to be puzzled by the promise of the progressive nature of the disease. "What stage am I in? Am I worse than I was a year ago? Why are some days better than others?" These are questions that plague every one of us.

h·o·p·e·

IS

FOR

HELP

Y ou can decide to go it alone. But it is so much more comforting to have a crew of supporters in your camp. After the initial shock of the diagnosis had diminished, I was ready to talk. The first person I wanted as a Parkinson's partner was Peggy, my wife.

I didn't want pity. I didn't want sympathy or any "poor me" talk. I wanted her to understand what Parkinson's was doing to my body, physically and emotionally. So we agreed to become partners in educating ourselves. We figured the unknown can create uncontrollable monsters that lead to misinformation, poor communications, and eventually depression. Also, we had seen some spouses and other family members begin to treat the Parkinson's Person as if they were suddenly "fragile" or a "sad case." The result was the Parkinson's Person wound up feeling guilty, stigmatized, demeaned, or worse—feeling sorry for themselves. Peggy and I agreed we'd have to do five things if we were to have a healthy existence with our new-found friend.

These were:

1. I wouldn't use her as a crutch. I would try to button all the buttons on my shirts. I would try to unlock the doors with my keys. I would try to use the screwdriver when called upon. Only when I felt it was extremely frustrating or it just wasn't going to happen would I call upon her for help.

21

2. I would be honest with her when she asked, "How are you doing?" We agreed it would help her better understand where I'm coming from as the condtions changed from day to day. I agreed to accept her offer of, "How can I help?" as team commitment, and not as a sympathetic gesture.

3. I agreed to accept her coaching suggestions without being irritated. "Pull your shoulders back." "Stand up straight." "You're mumbling." "I can't read your writing." Those were tips I had to get used to. But I had the option to call time out and say, "Hold up, I've had enough coaching for now."

4. I would not burden Peggy with having her constantly check to see if I had taken my medication. It was my responsibility. Not Peggy's.

5. I would not rely on Peggy to be my spokesperson. She would be supportive. But I should be accountable for expressing myself. (Too often we have observed the spouse speaking up almost as though the Parkinson's Person no longer had a thought in the world.)

From the first day I heard the words from my neurologist, "You have Parkinson's," Peggy and I have been active accumulators of facts about the disease. In five years, we have filled a file cabinet with articles, booklets, newsletters, computer printouts and video tapes. This has helped immensely in giving us encouragement that Parkinson's People can enjoy an active, vibrant quality of life. We have accumulated numerous personal accounts of people who are successfully coping with the troublesome symptoms of the disease. As you can see, there is quite a bit of Sue's attitude in my approach to life with this disease.

AN ENCOURAGING SIGN

One note that I have blown up in giant-size type in that file drawer reads as follows: YOUR CHANCES OF DYING OF NATURAL CAUSES ARE MUCH GREATER THAN DYING FROM PARKINSON'S DISEASE. We picked up that information from a neurologist's talk at a support group meeting. It gives me *hope* and reconfirms that living with Parkinson's doesn't have to be a killer of a job.

THE LETTER

I also involved my four children and their spouses. I called them on the phone and briefly explained the diagnosis. I told them they would be receiving a letter that explained how I needed their help. The letter I wrote is on the following pages.

23

To: *My Family*
From: *Hal/Dad/Grandpa*
Subject: *Medical Report*

You have been concerned about my right arm and how I carry my hand. I have told you that the stiffness was caused by my recent long bicycle trip. After much urging by some of you to have a medical examination, I have followed your wise direction. As is my style, I thought I could whip myself back to normal with extra exercise and will power. Not so, this time.

I have been to a hand specialist and have taken a number of tests. She referred me to a neurologist. The neurologist determined that the bike trip had nothing to do with my stiff arm swing and curled fingers. He arranged for an MRI test of my brain. The report was negative—no sign of stroke or brain tumor.

However, his diagnosis is that I am in the early stages of Parkinson's Disease.

I'd like to tell you what little I know about the disease and how you can help. But first, I'd like to emphasize that I have a positive attitude about my condition. If I do have it (the doctor says he's 80% sure), it can be effectively treated but not cured. It's not life threatening. Drugs can slow the process down, and in many cases improve mobility.

Parkinson's is caused by a deficiency of the brain to produce adequate amounts of the chemical dopamine. The chemical works hand in hand with the nervous system. When the brain lacks proper amounts of dopamine, several things can happen. The classic triad is tremor, rigidity and slow movement of certain parts of the body. Right now I don't have a tremor in my hand except for sometimes when I'm eating some of Mother's homemade soup. My arm is a little rigid and I have a problem swinging it naturally when I walk.

Another give-away is my handwriting. Some days I can write quite legibly. Other days I find it hard to form letters and the writing is very small.

For several months my speech has been soft. I tend to mumble. One symptom of Parkinson's is a monotone. This can be improved with drugs. (Mother tells me she's already noticed a change for the better.)

I don't plan to alter my lifestyle. I'll still run, ski, hike, bike, drive, work in the yard and continue to love every minute of being with all the members of the family.

What can you do to help? You can help me by reminding me to speak up when I wimp out my sentences. You can help me by talking about Parkinson's and not being fearful of offending me. You can help me by not worrying about the long-range consequences. I'm pleased it's not anything more serious and to have you overly concerned would create an unfair relationship.

The cause of Parkinson's is unknown. From all reports to date it is not a disease that is passed on through heredity. New *drugs are under study. Mother and I plan to learn everything possible about the old and new treatments. And I promise to give you an honest report on my condition.*

Thanks for your help.

OPENING UP TO THE FAMILY

As you can readily see there's a little of Jack, Sue, Carl, and Bill all wrapped up in the letter. Its intent was to explain the new situation I would be living with daily, and to open up the avenues of conversation. I didn't want a hush-hush environment. My daughter shed a few tears and was compassionate. My three sons tried to conceal their concern with analytical questions. I had to remember they had to get used to the idea of their father having a health change that could get worse. They needed time to grieve, to work through their fears and to get angry if they needed to. After all, they had grown up with a father who skied with them, hiked the mountains with them, built tree houses with them, played on the beach with them and had done a thousand things that ordinary fathers do with their children. It took some time to get used to the idea that their image of a bulletproof father was changing.

Now I find that they call me up and say, "I met a guy who has just been diagnosed with Parkinson's. I think you should talk to him." Or I'll get a call with the message, "I just read an article in the newspaper about Parkinson's and I'm sending it to you." I tell them about new developments in medications, new treatments, and the experiences I've had with other Parkinson's people. I try not to dwell on my condition. I figure my children shouldn't have to hear about Dad's or Mom's health for more than a few minutes at a time. I consider my family members an integral part of the *hope* team. Peggy and I are not alone with the disease. And the family is not alone imagining all sorts of wild stories about my outcome.

Even though I am open about my Parkinson's, I sometimes catch my family members studying me. It's done in a casual but scrutinizing manner. They're eying me for any changes that may have taken place since we last got together. The natural impulse is to pull the shoulders back, straighten up and try to be more erect, along with trying to show that I'm flexible, not stiff or rigid. The only person I tend to fool is myself. Because they've already formed an opinion.

I often ask, "Do you see any difference in me since you last saw me?" That's a question you have to have courage to throw into the air and you have to be willing to accept a possible, "Yes, I do." Sometimes I hear: "You look more bent over," or "Your face seems more frozen." But generally I get positive feedback. These check-ins are important communication steps for me because it involves those I love in the process of *hope.*

h·o·p·e·

BEING HONEST

It's important that the family doesn't have whisper campaigns about the Parkinson's Person. If there are concerns, they should be addressed. And the person living with Parkinson's needs to be receptive and most of all, not defensive. At the same time, the Parkinson Person must be honest with his or her health reports. I'm guilty of always wanting to convey up-beat news—"I walked five miles in the rain." "I biked Madrona hill today." "I hiked up Mt. Si on Sunday." I should also be more willing to say, "I'm having a little difficulty with a frozen mouth and I mumble." Or "I wish I didn't have the stone face so much." I have to remember that you can't hide much with Parkinson's. That was brought home to me when my grandchild asked, "Grandpa, why do you always look so sad?" A three year old had picked up my stoic face, and was troubled about the change. That was the time I had to give my explanation of Parkinson's to a preschooler. The best I could come up with was, "Grandpa has a sickness in his brain that keeps him from smiling. He's really happy on the inside. He just can't show it on the outside."

KNOWING WHEN YOU NEED HELP

Calling for help takes maturity with the disease. Particularly if you've pledged to try your darnedest to be self-sufficient. Like

28

Jack, I have become less proficient with a screwdriver. I don't have the strength in my right hand to twist a screw or to hold the head in place. Ten years ago I built a vacation cabin. Working virtually alone I had done all the electrical wiring, plumbing and interior woodwork. It was a satisfying creative project requiring lots of hand skills. Recently, I had to wire the cabin for a clothes dryer. In the pre-Parkinson's days it would have been a snap. Not so on this chosen day. After several hours of working in close quarters and fighting with a junction box, I finally realized I wasn't going to get the screwdriver to do its job. I needed help. And I asked Peggy if she would finish up the task. In the early days of my diagnosis, that would have been ego-destroying. Now I accept what I can't do as part of living with the conditions of the disease. I figure, next time, maybe the screwdriver will work a little better for me. It usually does. And that gives me *hope.*

LIVING WITH THE AVERAGES

Sometimes the buttons on a shirt will not cooperate. My left sleeve is always touch and go. About 80 percent of the time I can make it happen. In baseball that's .800, which is a phenomenal batting average. But in the game of Parkinson's an .800 average can be gut wrenching. I face each day not knowing whether the little button will go into the little hole or not. Some days require as many as 15 attempts before success. Other days there's a connection on the first try. Peggy will see me struggling but follows our agreement: It's my responsibility to do it alone if possible. However, it's extremely comforting to know I can trust her for help when the repeated attempts become too frustrating. If the average drops to 50%, then I'll have to face that day.

Which brings up an important point—<u>You have the power to control your thoughts. If you think negatively, chances are you will wind up fulfilling your most dreaded wishes while living a life of hell before you get there. If you think positively it will keep you active and involved with life and the chances are much greater that you just might change your outcome for the better.</u> And that is consistent with the concept of *hope.*

WHAT ABOUT YOUR WORK PLACE?

It's a big decision as to whether you confide in your employer that you have Parkinson's. Bill was fearful that his tremor would give him away. He failed to recognize that he had an understanding boss. But no matter how compassionate an employer may be, the Parkinson's Person will still have to be judged on the merits of his or her performance, just like any other employee. If the disease limits the person, we can't expect the employer to overlook the reduction in daily output.

Before you tell your employer about your new health problem, it would be a good idea to do an objective assessment of what you can successfully accomplish and just what responsibilities you will be sub-par in performing. Chances are that you'll still be able to meet the requirements of your job description.

After you've completed your analysis, ask yourself: "If I were boss and someone with my condition came to me with an evaluation like this, would it make any difference in my attitude toward their ability to perform their job?" Trying to make a secret out of your condition is probably a mistake. Chances are high that the people in your office or in the field have already noticed some subtle changes in your physical condition.

If you decide it's important to inform your boss, I suggest you prepare a one page explanation of your condition. Arrange an appointment and go over the statement you have prepared with him or her. An example of how one person handled the statement follows:

Dear Stanley:

On Tuesday, July 9th I was told by my neurologist that I have Parkinson's Disease. It was once considered an elderly person's disease. But it is now being diagnosed in the younger generations. In fact, in the U. S. there are 1,500,000 people who have Parkinson's.

<u>What is Parkinson's?</u> There is a tiny portion of the brain that produces dopamine which acts as a chemical messenger, sending signals to the nerve cells. When the brain is unable to produce sufficient amounts of dopamine, several things may happen: there may be a tremor, there may be muscular stiffness or there may be slowness in body movement. There is no impairment in ability to think or reason clearly. My symptoms are: 1) I have a slight trembling in my left hand; 2) I am a little stooped when I walk; 3) my handwriting is smaller than it used to be.

<u>What is the cause of Parkinson's?</u> No one is quite sure. Research has revealed it could be caused by chemicals in well water or pesticides. It is not life threatening but it is progressive. And it affects everyone in different ways.

<u>How does Parkinson's affect my work?</u> It doesn't affect my ability to solve problems. Medication helps control the involuntary trembling of my left hand. I am taking physical therapy classes to help correct my posture. I am exercising my hand to resolve the muscular stiffness that causes such small handwriting and affects my word processing efficiency.

I don't anticipate any problem areas in fulfilling my work responsibilities.

<u>What I would like.</u> I would like to be considered a vital and important employee even though I have Parkinson's—by my co-workers and by management. I do not want any special treatment or to be labeled as handicapped.

<u>What you can expect of me.</u> A commitment to do a first-rate job. Loyalty to the company. Openness about my condition to fellow employees. And periodic reports to you on my condition.

Sincerely,
Ann Smith

What you want out of the meeting is a confirmation that your boss is in agreement that you can continue to do the job you've been assigned. If your boss has any hesitation or outright concerns, they should be addressed at this meeting. The usual reaction from your superior will be sympathy–"I'm sorry to hear that, Ann." It's nice to have a compassionate boss, but you need some definition as to your future status with the firm. Chances are you will hear, "Let's just see how things progress." If your boss says, "I have seen your tremor and wondered about it," you might ask, "Is it offensive to you?" You might also ask, "Now that you know I have Parkinson's, does that change your attitude about my future with the company?" Don't be confrontational or appear anxious. Naturally, your company will be concerned about any commitment that will be legally binding.

THE ROLE OF A SUPPORT GROUP

When I was first diagnosed, I wasn't ready for a support group. The term conjured up an image of lots of needy people droning on about their aches, pains and worries. I couldn't conceive how listening to this crowd of "sickies" could help me. This seems to be a common reaction among a high percentage of Parkinson's people. It certainly was the attitude of Jack, Sue, Carl and Bill.

How Peggy and I got involved in a support group was really quite natural. I had talked with a friend who had recently been diagnosed with Parkinson's. We exchanged information about our symptoms, medication, doctors, feelings, downers, uppers and all the usual things that Parkinson's People wind up talking about. Then one day his wife called and said, "We've been to a support group and I think it would interest you. There are a lot of bright, active and sensitive people in the group." I said, "Let me think about it." Peggy and I discussed it and agreed we'd try it. During the first session we attended I learned that I might be going to the wrong neurologist. Carin, the support group leader, commented sometime during the session that when you have Parkinson's you should be under the treatment of a Parkinson's specialist—someone whose primary practice is Parkinson's. I asked, "How do you determine that?" Her simple reply was, "You ask the doctor, 'How many Parkinson's patients do you treat?'" Her additional advice was: "You ask the doctor about new medications." "If you get a fuzzy answer, then chances are you may not have a specialist who is up-to-date on how to make your quality of life the best it can be." Her counsel set me on a path of *hope.*

THE SUPPORT GROUP CHANGED MY LIFE

During my next doctor's visit I asked, "How many Parkinson's patients do you have?" The man in the white coat gazed at the ceiling as he thought about the question and finally replied, "Including you, about eight or nine." That told me I might be getting more help from a specialist who had 10 or 20 times that number. The answer to the follow-up question was the real clincher. I asked, "I've read about a drug called Mirapex, do you think that would help me?" He replied, "You've got me on that one. I don't know much about it."

I learned from the support group members who they felt were the Parkinson's specialists in the area. From their recommendations, I hooked up with a neurologist in which I developed complete confidence. She has given me *hope.* Had

I continued with the same doctor, I'm sure my improvement would have been limited to the doctor's restricted knowledge. That's not to say my former neurologist wasn't a competent doctor. There are dozens of neurological specialties—it just so happened that he didn't concentrate in movement disorders.

The support group has given me help, and consequently *hope,* in the following ways:

1. The exchange of information between Parkinson's People is of tremendous benefit—medication information, exercise tricks, new developments, doctor relations, and an opportunity to get genuine feedback from people who are facing similar problems day-in and day-out. For example:

    "I break my Sinemet in half and take one half when I first awaken in the morning. Then I take the other half an hour later, just before I exercise. This seems to kick-start me."

    "Has anybody had dizziness or disorientation when they get up at night? What do you do about it?"

    "I find that my neurologist spends more time with me if I write down the three things I want him to discuss with me during my visit—listing the primary concern first."

2. The first-hand experiences of Parkinson's people

who are living a quality life (not merely existing) stimulates a positive outlook on the future and prevents me from getting caught up in the "worry wart" attitude.

"I missed the last meeting because I was on a cruise to Alaska. Seemed like the medication had longer 'on' periods than when I was home."

"When I hike in the woods I never seem to stumble, but when I'm walking on a shopping mall marble floor I trip every now and then. If I could always pick up my feet like I do in the forest, I'd be a whiz."

"I find that when I stand in line at the bank or grocery store, if I put my hands on my hips, it pulls my shoulders back."

3. A network of common interest is built so there is a natural exchange of encouragement and care.

"I feel I can express my personal concerns openly, and every member of the support group will listen. It gives me a sounding board that I need periodically."

"I have gained the understanding that there is a Parkinson community of friends, doctors, family members, and specialists who are unified in their concerns for my problems. In other words, I'm not alone with my disease."

"I thought I was the only one having troubles with soft voice and halting speech until I listened to the other members of my group. I've picked up some good pointers."

4. It is tremendously informative to have neurologists, speech specialists, physical therapists, and other guest speakers explain treatments and causes of the uniqueness of this diseases.

"I save all the handouts and brochures. I find them to be especially helpful resource pieces."

"I never miss a meeting when we have a guest speaker. The information is priceless."

"I get to ask questions of the specialists. It's like having a personal advisor on hand to give me counsel. It also keeps me up-to-date on the new advances in treatment."

WHAT MAKES A SUPPORT GROUP HUM

If you decide to attend a support group, make sure there is variety in the sessions. Guest speakers are essential to keeping the group alive and vital. Chances are you won't want to sit in a circle meeting after meeting and listen to each other expound on symptoms and side effects. Be instrumental in making sure outside professionals make up at least one-half of your sessions. These speakers can bring great *hope* to the group. Suggestions for speakers and participants are: neurologists, physical therapists, speech therapists, exercise specialists, naturopaths, travel agents, sleep disorder specialists, pharmacists, health insurance experts, ophthalmologists, and legal planners. Just to name a few. If you know of someone who is living with Parkinson's and can impart vitality and courage into your group, ask them to be a guest speaker. The network of *hope* will grow as you make more and more contacts. Be pro-active. Don't wait for "things" to happen. And don't be fearful of having fun. Laughter uses many more muscles than sitting.

How do you learn about a nearby support group? Contact the following organizations: American Parkinson's Disease Association; National Parkinson's Foundation; or Northwest Parkinson's Foundation. All three organizations sponsor and are actively involved with support groups. Addresses, web site information and telephone numbers are listed later. A reliable resource is an attendee of a local support group. If you know someone who has Parkinson's, find out if they attend a Support Group. Ask them how active the group is and what you can expect if you show up. Then give it a try. You are not committing yourself for life. You are simply testing the waters.

FINDING A PARKINSON'S FRIEND

You may decide that support groups are not your cup of tea. In that case I would strongly urge you to make contact with someone else who has Parkinson's, preferably a person who will be a good listener—someone you'll also be willing to listen to. Chances are you'll have "downer days" from time to time, and it's refreshing to have a sympathetic cohort who really understands what you're talking about when you say, "I've been so tired the last couple of days. I wonder if I'm on the right dosage of medication. Have you had periods when you can't get charged up?" Your Parkinson's friend has probably been there too.

It's such a relief to have an exchange with someone who has experienced your experience. Suddenly, you're not alone. I guarantee you, it's not the same as discussing it with your spouse or with a non-Parkinson's person. Of course, it's a two-way street. You have to be willing to listen to your partner's concerns too and not be a parasite. Sometimes your shared concerns will stimulate wonderful conversations in which you both benefit.

How do you find partners you can call on? When I was diagnosed with Parkinson's, I didn't know a single person with

the disease. Or so I thought. Peggy and I attended a seminar given by a local hospital. That day I encountered two friends I hadn't seen in years who had Parkinson's. I had a former business acquaintance I hadn't seen in 20 years call up and say, "I hear you have Parkinson's. So do I." I have friends call me and say, "I have a golfing buddy who was just diagnosed with Parkinson's. Would you mind talking to him?" I've had people I didn't know call me to say they were referred by so-and-so and wanted to know if I thought they were on the right medication. I always preface my comments with, "I'm not a physician and you should rely on your physician for medical advice. But I <u>can</u> speak of my own experiences with various dosages and medications." Parkinson's People are hungry for information and companionship. It's a sure thing—make an open acknowledgement that you have Parkinson's, and you'll be surprised how the network of *hope* will reach you and reveal new-found partners.

THE TRUE MEANING OF HELP

The H letter in the promise of *hope* is HELP. Not a cry for "Help!" like an SOS. But an involvement with your spouse, your partner, your family and friends so that they appreciate what you are experiencing and can respond naturally. I can think of two incidents that help to make this point. One is when I was fishing a stream with my friend, Neil. The salmon were hitting my lure like it was the only meal left in this world. I had just lost a big one and was trying to retie a leader. Neil looked over and saw my fumbling fingers. He just quietly said, "Here, hold my pole a second." He then proceeded to skillfully do what I was having so much difficulty doing. He handed me back my pole and I gave him his. I thanked him. He smiled as if to say, "Glad to help." It seemed like the natural thing for one friend to do for another.

Another incident occurred at a hospital board meeting. I was to give a simple report on some new equipment the hospital was using. I started out mumbling and got my words so twisted around I had to defer to the hospital CEO to explain what I was assigned to do. I simply said, "I have Parkinson's and sometimes I have trouble speaking. I'm going to ask Paul to fill in for me." In pre-Parkinson's days it would have been a snap. I was used to speaking and was proud of my ability to ad-lib. But that day I sounded like a four year old delivering a speech on the economy of Nepal. I sat down discouraged that Parkinson's had played a surprising trick on me. The chief of staff, a good doctor friend, slipped me a note. It read "Hal, you do a super job. Don't let PD get you down. We need you. Fred." It was a timely piece of encouragement from a good friend. And a big help to a bruised ego.

I AM SMILING

I have one more story before we go on to explore the O in the word *hope*. I had been assigned the job of planning a reunion of college friends. They were unaware of my Parkinson's diagnosis. I hadn't seen many of them for years. So I took a minute to explain the reason that I didn't smile like I used to. I wanted them to understand that my stoic face was not a sign of boredom or sadness. I didn't dwell on it. I merely called it to their attention. The reunion trip was on the Holland-America cruise ship to Alaska. My college buddies picked up on my concern about looking too serious and each night at dinner someone would say, "Smile, damn it." I would reply: "I <u>am</u> smiling." I appreciated the openness and the fact that my old friends felt they could call 'em as they see 'em without being disrespectful.

One night in Sitka I was surprised by a gift from one of the members of the group. I opened the package and found a black t-shirt. On the front of the shirt was a giant eagle with a stern look as though he were angry with all living creatures. Above the tough old bird was the statement, "I <u>am</u> smiling!" Charlie had found the shirt at the Sitka Raptor Center and thought it was most appropriate for me. I value that shirt for what it represents—by being up front with my friends there was no wondering, whispering or out-of-bounds comments regarding my condition. The incident was also a great help in reminding me that laughter is one of the best medications you can have for a serious disease such as Parkinson's.

HELP IS EVERYWHERE YOU LOOK

Help comes in many ways. It can be from your spouse, or care giver, or significant other, or children, or friend(s), or a neighbor, or a stranger. If you are open and straightforward about your condition, you'll be amazed what loving support will prevail. It may be a gentle tug on the shoulder by a friend who hasn't seen you for some time with his kind query, "How you doing?" It's your friend's way of saying, "I've been thinking about you." It may be a telephone call from a grandchild who simply says, "Grandpa, how are you feeling?" Or else a neighbor who drops in to bring you some fresh garden flowers. This HELP is executed in love. Take it in. Enjoy its spiritual power to make you feel important to life. Suddenly you are not alone. You'll discover you can laugh, express joy, breathe deeper, walk a little taller, maybe even hum a favorite tune and forget for a moment the physical woes you are dealing with each day.

h·o·p·e·

IS

FOR

OPTIMISM

Depression can be an ugly cohort of Parkinson's Disease. About 60% of Parkinson's people have periods when they feel dejected, out of sorts or have more chronic symptoms of hopelessness for extended periods of time. This means that six out of ten will have what may be called clinical depression (not just being "burned-out"). There can be bereavement over the loss of personal dreams. There can be embarrassment over the loss of the "vital self." There can be anger and the "why me" attitude that can often make a person lose their zest for life. There can be ambivalence where the Parkinson's Person wraps himself or herself into a self-protective blanket of "yes, but" and "it's no use" responses.

This depression can be helped by some very effective and highly recommended drugs. Sometimes medication is essential. Sometimes it's not.

I've found that my Parkinson's Disease is an up-and-down affair. And this seems to hold true for many of my friends with Parkinson's. One day you feel like your old self. The next day you're slow, stiff, uninspired, and act 20 years older. This can even happen to me within the same day. I can be a tiger at 7 a.m. and a sloth at noon. Some days I can feel energized at noon and at 4 p.m. feel like I have the flu.

ACCEPTANCE IS CRITICAL

Remember Bill, the angry one? He was determined he could beat the disease. This is an attitude that is destined to lead to depression. <u>You</u> can't control this disease. There's no way you can anticipate and react normally to the changes that take place in that tiny mass in your brain called the substantia nigra. There are "highs" and "lows," and "offs" and "ons" as the body responds to an unpredictable flow of dopamine to the nerve cells. Medication will help. Diet will help. Exercise will help. Attitude will help. But the biggest hurdle for a newly diagnosed Parkinson's Person is accepting the idea that your body will not be the same as it was before.

How can you be optimistic under such conditions? I have a doctor friend who has treated thousands of Parkinson's People. His advice is: "Accommodate the disorder but do not surrender to it. Take on an attitude that tells your body 'I will not be defeated.'" In his years of experience with Parkinson's People, he is convinced that attitude plays a major role in determining the quality of life, and the general health of the individual. Those who fight the disease every step of the way are formulating a pathway to frustration, depression, and unhappiness.

REASONS TO BE POSITIVE

First, you can be thankful that you don't have a life-threatening diagnosis. People don't die from Parkinson's disease. Your doctor won't predict you have only six months to live. Nor will you need a complicated surgery right off the bat. Parkinson's People have lived 30 or 40 additional years without altering their quality of life too drastically. Sure, it's an inconvenience and an unfortunate draw of the cards, but it could be worse.

Second, you can be thankful that there are many medication choices that are working well for Parkinson's People who have a variety of symptoms. If you had been faced with the diagnosis 15 years ago, your options would have been drastically limited. Working with a Parkinson's specialist, chances are high that you can find the right medication solution that will give you a more optimistic outlook on your daily life and the future. Further encouragement is that more and more money is going into research to find a cure, into making the quality of life better, and into determining the cause of the disease. In addition, specialized Parkinson's clinics offer you comprehensive evaluations of medications, physical therapy, voice improvement, nutritional recommendations, and care giver training.

Third, there is a wealth of information available on the subject of Parkinson's Disease. Knowledge of what you have and how it works is vital to understanding what lies ahead for you. Two books I recommend are:

Parkinson's Disease
The Complete Guide for Patients and Care Givers
by Dr. Abraham N. Lieberman and Dr. Frank L. Williams

Parkinson's Disease
A Guide for Patient and Family
by Dr. Roger C. Duvoisin

These are two standbys. Your local bookstore will have many other choices in its Health Section.

I suggest you read these two books before you go to the internet to resource information. A fundamental understanding will help you filter out the "hoped-for truths" and the "real thing." What these two books did for me was to give me reassurance that I can improve some of the functional limitations of my Parkinson's. In more plain English, the authors gave me *hope* and in turn I immediately felt more optimistic.

There are three other sources of information that I rely on:

Northwest Parkinson's Foundation (NWPF)
1206 123rd Ave. SE
Bellevue, WA 98005   www.nwpf.org

National Parkinson's Foundation (NPF)
1501 NW Ninth Avenue/Bob Hope Road
Miami, FL 33136   www.parkinson.org

American Parkinson's Disease Association (APDA)
1250 Hylan Blvd
Suite 4B
Staten Island, NY 10305   www.apdaparkinson.com

All three produce periodic publications that are excellent information resources. Some examples of booklets that are available from NPF are: <u>Speaking Out</u>; <u>What You and Your Family Should Know</u>; <u>Fitness Counts</u>; <u>Medications</u>; and <u>Nutritional Matters</u>. The Northwest Parkinson's Foundation has a newsletter and a wonderful website that is up-to-date and loaded with interesting material. The Washington chapter of the APDA produces a newsletter called the <u>Pathfinder</u> which will keep you aware of local symposia and educational opportunities.

REMEMBER THE GOOD DAYS

You can read volumes about the disease and you can talk for hours about your similarities of symptoms with your Parkinson's friends, but living with the idiosyncratic nature and unpredictability of the disease is having to "walk the walk." I said earlier, you have to accept that your body will never be the same. That's critical. But it doesn't have to be a total downer.

If you're like most of us, you'll have days and periods of time when you feel "pretty good." Relish the good experiences. Learn how to tell someone, "I'm feeling good right now." Rather than being a broken record that sing-songs, "Gee, I feel awful" every time someone asks, "How 'ya doing?" I'm not asking you to be dishonest. I am suggesting that you savor the good periods so that they become more memorable than the bad times. Pile up "sunshine hours" rather than "monthly doldrums." To do this you need a reference point. I'll use a mountain climbing experience to make my point.

SETTING A REFERENCE POINT

Ten years before I was diagnosed with Parkinson's, Peggy and I went on an Outward Bound trip to climb Mt. Kilimanjaro. We were among a party of 55- to 65-year-olds who were being led by young Kenyans and American Outward Bound instructors. It's 19,340 vertical feet to the summit. We climbed the back side of the mountain, sleeping in caves and hiking through heather bushes that had been charred from burnings by poachers seeking wild game. It was tough going even at the lower elevations. As we reached the 10,000 foot level, our breathing became more difficult and the pace slowed. We slept the final night at 17,000 feet and arose at 2 a.m. to make the climb to the top of Africa. Our headlamps picked the way over scree that was piled a foot or so thick. This footing caused us to take two steps forward and then to slip back one. The air was thinner. Our lungs were burning. It was cold. Our water bottles froze. The wind was blowing 30 mph. We would rest periodically and hold on to each other for warmth. It was one small step after one small step. I thought the summit was running away from us. Finally, we all made it and found ourselves looking down into the crater. We were exhausted. But we made it.

Now when I am taxed to the point where I think I can't move another step or the task seems far over-whelming, I recall that day on Kilimanjaro. That was one of the toughest experiences in my life. So far, any Parkinson's symptom I've had hasn't been as difficult as the physical abuse I put my body through on the mountain. This is my reference point. It gives me optimism. It gives me *hope*.

KEEP YOUR GOALS ALIVE

I began biking when running became more difficult. First I biked around the neighborhood just to get the hang of it.

Then I upped it to an hour adventure to new parts of the city. Soon I was covering 30 miles in a morning session. It was an exciting experience. I couldn't get the leg turnover that the sleek racers were getting and I didn't have the skintight flashy jersey. As a matter of fact, it seemed like everybody whizzed past me—even little old ladies with a basketful of groceries on the rear of their bikes. But I didn't seem to care. I was having fun. Then a goal popped into the picture. I read about the Seattle to Portland (STP) Bike Event—a 200 mile ride with 8000 participants. A group was forming called Team Parkinson's. There were 40 riders who were committed to raise money for the Northwest Parkinson's Foundation. I knew I could ride 30 miles, but 200 was a challenge. Before I bit the bullet, I tested my endurance. I wasn't sure I could handle two days of pedaling hills and highways. One day I managed to cover 100 miles in about eight hours, with "several" rest stops. The next day I signed up for Team Parkinson's. My goal was to complete the 200 mile journey in two days. I knew it would be intense, but I set a goal—To Make It Without Having To Push My Bike Up Any Hills. I didn't have any time goal or speed goal. It was simply to complete the 200 miles.

Fortunately, I had five support riders that gave me encouragement every turn of the pedal. Bill, Craig, Margo, Dave, and Scott were with me throughout the trip. All were riding for Team Parkinson's. All were tuned to a pace that was comfortable for me. All were willing to hold back—even though they could have finished well before we rolled into Portland where a band was playing and finishers were lounging on the grass. I met my goal. It has done wonders for my self esteem. So now when I'm having a shuffling day of slowness I remember the STP experience—with good friends and a sense of accomplishment. It proved to me that goal setting should not be disregarded simply because I have Parkinson's. They don't have to be giant physical endeavors. They can be simple achievements—improve your putting on the golf course, clean up your workbench, grow a vegetable garden, reorganize your family pictures, or find that valuable antique you've desired for so many years. Goal-setting is one of the keys to *optimism.* As long as you set realistic goals, you will find it does two things: 1) it gets your mind off your Parkinson's condition; and 2) it is a valuable confidence builder.

WHEN THE GOING GETS TOUGH

I encourage you to pick an incident in your lifetime that was particularly emotionally or physically challenging—something over which you triumphed. Make a mental recording of what your body was experiencing at that time. Use it as your reference point. Then, when you are having a particularly "down hour" or "down day," compare it to <u>your</u> reference point. It doesn't have to be a physical endeavor. It could be an emotional period in your life—an adjustment to being a high school teenager; a marriage separation; loss of a job and a difficult employment search; or a confrontation with a friend that was never resolved. However, since the symptoms of Parkinson's often are predominately physical, it is best that you select some difficult incident of exertion in your past.

I use my Kilimanjaro and STP biking references when running. Now that I have Parkinson's, I've slowed down quite a bit. I have trouble sustaining a three mile run. My legs tire after about one mile. I have to walk for a block or so and then I can pick up the running again. Then they tire. And I walk. I am determined to keep going for three miles. It's just like climbing Kilimanjaro or biking the hills outside Portland. Only easier. But it's still tough. I could quit after one mile. Or I could do nothing. I have learned that the accomplishment of finishing three miles is emotionally and physically rewarding. I will continue to use the three miles as a goal until my doctor says, "You had better knock it off."

DON'T QUIT

I've seen far too many of my Parkinson's friends quit when the effort seemed overwhelming. They didn't seem to have a reference point. And what happens is that they "stop doing" all together. Giving up golf because your swing isn't just right or you tire walking the course is giving up the optimistic side of your life. Giving up walking because you get out of breath is giving up a component of the better quality of life. If your doctor says you shouldn't do it because it might endanger your health, that's a different story. But when you quit just because it seems a little tougher, you are penalizing a vital part of *hope*—optimism. When you believe in a favorable outcome, rather than a failure, you are on target to a better quality of life.

SOME SUGGESTIONS

Think of the opposite position—pessimism. If you believe you are getting worse by the day or minute, you can accelerate your stiffness, your tremor, your freezing, your despondency and your attitude about a negative future. You can't order someone to be optimistic and expect immediate results. But there are some actions that you can take to encourage optimism. Here are ten ideas to think about:

1. <u>Enjoy the moment.</u> Don't dwell on what's going to happen to you in the future. Sure, Parkinson's is a progressive disease. But you have no way of determining what stage you'll be in five, ten or fifteen years from now. Maybe they'll find a cure in the next few years. Then you have worried for nothing.

2. <u>Be a ring leader for laughter.</u> Surround yourself with happy, upbeat people. Love a good joke—and don't be shy about laughing about your Parkinson's experiences.

3. <u>Have at least three things you do well.</u> It could be cooking, bridge, golf, painting, crosswords, reading, hiking, walking, etc. When you have a trio of activities then you are not focused in on a single skill. When you are not doing well in one, you can always turn to the other two.

4. <u>Be active.</u> Don't sit. Keep moving even though you may not feel like it at times.

5. <u>Take time to rest</u> (after you've done No. 4). Parkinson's tires the body because it requires more energy than you needed before.

6. <u>Believe in yourself.</u> When you say "I can't" more often than you say "I'll try" or "I will" then you are endangering your growth and narrowing your horizons. Keep score of the number of times a day you say, "I can't." How many of these "I can'ts" are cop outs?

7. <u>Have balance in your life.</u> Be knowledgeable about Parkinson's but don't spend 24 hours each day wrapped up in the disease. Don't become an Internet Junkie constantly looking for a breakthrough in the disease or talking for hours in chat rooms.

8. <u>Volunteer to help someone else</u> or get involved in a worthwhile cause. Giving your time and energy can be a real boost to your self worth. There are hundreds of non-profit organizations in your area that could use some of your talents.

9. <u>Don't hole up.</u> When your spirits are low, call a good friend for coffee. See an upbeat movie. Get out of the routine you've been following for the past few days.

10. <u>Be adventuresome.</u> Take risks. Try something you've been fearful of doing. Maybe it's time to ride a bicycle. Or take a hike in the woods. Go to an ice rink. What about bungee jumping? This can be a big challenge, but the rewards are huge.

REFUSE TO LOSE

Many sports teams have fans that support their heroes with signs that say REFUSE TO LOSE. These tend to show up in the bleachers during the playoffs, when the underdog is fighting for survival. The confidence grows, the players perform beyond what is considered humanly possible and suddenly there is a belief that the championship is achievable. I think REFUSE TO LOSE is an appropriate objective for the newly diagnosed Parkinson's Person. If you adopt the attitude that you will REFUSE TO LOSE, it will do wonders for your optimism. You may have progressive symptoms over the years ahead, but you don't have to lose your dignity, self-respect or sense of value to your community and family. Don't let Parkinson's take charge of your attitude. You can be in charge of what you think, <u>how</u> you think, and whether you elect to have a positive outlook or not. Make it a daily pledge to refuse to lose your optimism.

TAKE THE RISK

Remember when you were a little squirt and you were holding onto the edge of the pool? If you let go, the water would be over your head. Your parents kept encouraging you to let go, and stroke with your arms and kick your feet. They would say, "You can do it." But you thought, "I'll sink and swallow water and maybe drown." You would let go with one hand, and almost take the plunge, but at the last moment fear would take hold and you'd once again cling to the security of the pool edge. You saw other kids splashing and floating so you knew it was possible. Finally you pushed off and let go. At first you frantically kicked and moved your arms. You didn't sink. You were swimming. You were on your way. Each time you entered the pool your confidence grew. The fear of failure turned into optimism. It also became fun as you ventured farther and farther into the water. This experience is much like taking on the challenges you face with Parkinson's. If you hang onto the edge of the pool and never let go, you'll never experience the success of living a quality of life that is filled with optimism. You'll be amazed at what you can accomplish even though you have Parkinson's. Let go!

THE TOMORROW TRAP

Optimism is an illusive component of *hope.* There are bound to be periods when your spirits aren't up to par. There will be times when you just don't feel well. Some days you'd rather sit than walk. I find that when such "setbacks" occur, it requires special effort to complete tasks. There's a tendency to put off projects—"I'll clean off the workbench next week." "I'll vacuum the house tomorrow." "I'll trim the rose bushes next weekend." "I'll wash the car after the next rain." "I'll get to typing that report tomorrow." Do those statements sound familiar? I recommend that you don't fall into the trap of "Tomorrow. Tomorrow." Because "Tomorrow" will eat away your optimism. That's one of the great evils of this disease. It lulls you into thinking you don't have the energy to accomplish anything right now. You'll be so proud of yourself when you see what can be done, even though your mind and body are saying, "Let's sit this one out."

There will be times when you <u>should</u> rest—when your body is saying it's tired and your movements are slower. What I have to be careful about is being deceived into non-action when I <u>am</u> capable of performing physical activity.

THE CASE OF THE FUMBLING WALLET

I have poor finger dexterity in my right hand. This can cause an embarrassing delay at the hardware store, or anywhere there might be a line of people waiting to check out. I have found myself fumbling for bills in my wallet as I tried to pay the cashier the designated amount. And then there was the frustration of trying to return bills to my wallet. I used to be quite nervous about holding up people. The solution was quite simple. I carry several $20 bills in my wallet. Most things that I purchase are under $20. If my charge is $11.32, I hand the clerk one of the $20's. I don't try and put the change of three one dollar bills and the five dollar bill into my wallet while checking out. I put the bills and coins in my pocket and then go through the slow process of loading my wallet while in the car. This prevents a delay in the checkout line and the questioning stares. I wind up with a drawer full of change and lots of bills that I cash in for twenties at the bank. But it gives me optimism that I will be able to handle what could be a frustrating experience.

MR. "T"

How can you be optimistic when your tremor is giving you fits? I have a friend who is in the early stage of Parkinson's. He calls his tremor Mr. T. He talks to Mr. T. from time to time. He's on a friendly relationship with Mr. T. because Mr. T. most often has the upper hand. He might say, "Mr. T., I see you're shaking quite badly. What do you want?" Mr. T. could reply, "I'm dying for some more dopamine."

The conversation might go on as follows:

My friend: "I can't help you there. I'm not due for medication for another two hours."

Mr. T.: "Why don't you pick up that book over there and let me hold on. I think it will calm me down."

My friend: "Relax, Mr. T. Relax.

Mr. T.: "You relax, too. You're stiff as a board. Loosen up. You're making me nervous. And the tighter you get the more I can't control my shaking."

My friend: "How's that? Am I more loose?"

Mr. T: "Better. See. I am much calmer. Thanks for your help."

It may seem juvenile to carry on with an imaginary character, particularly one who is part of your physical self. But for my friend it works. By giving the tremor a personality, my friend has a communications vehicle to reason through a solution. It doesn't always work but it has a high success ratio. For my friend, he is optimistic that he can have some say in the outcome when the tremor occurs. He's not leaving it up to chance. He's taking charge. He's refusing to lose. Of course, his condition is not severe. He says if the tremor becomes more acute, he'll have to either talk faster or find a new solution. But he doesn't dwell on the negatives or worry about the uncertain future. He's living each day with an optimistic viewpoint.

The case I'm making is that if you elect to take on an optimistic attitude, you can find hundreds of ways to live with Parkinson's and enjoy a quality of life that is simply not possible with many other disorders. You can't expect to pile up a record of optimism for 24 hours a day, 365 days of the year. The very nature of the disease is that there are some good days and some bad days.

Learning to cope with these ups and downs is essential. There are bound to be some rough spots. Depression is a major concern for Parkinson's People. Medication can help here and we'll talk about that when we get to the physician section. But if you surround yourself with positive sensations in your daily endeavors, and commit to memory the good periods rather than bad, you are well on your way to finding optimism in your life.

h·o·p·e·

IS

FOR

PHYSICIAN

If you have a good physician the probability is high that you will have *hope* for a better quality of life. But it is essential that you have a doctor who is well versed in the administration of specific drugs that treat Parkinson's. It is desirable that you have a specialist in movement disorders. There's just too much happening in medications for anyone other than a specialist to keep up with the innovations and advancements in treatment. So if you have been diagnosed by a family doctor, internist, or general practitioner, ask him or her to recommend a neurologist who treats Parkinson's cases. Better yet, ask someone who has Parkinson's for a suggestion. Or call the Northwest Parkinson's Foundation and ask for a list of specialists.

MANY MEDICATION CHOICES

If you have to have Parkinson's, this is a good time to have it. Thirty years ago levodopa was about the only choice a physician had for the treatment of the disease. In that era, Parkinson's People were faced with one medication (levodopa) that often made them sick and left them wondering whether the pill that gave them some relief was worth the troublesome side effects. Today there are many options–carbidopa-levodopa, dopamine agonists, Mao-B inhibitors, COMT inhibitors, and anticholinergic agents. There are such trade names as Sinemet, Sinemet CR, Artane, Symmetrel, Parlodel, Mirapex,

Requip, Tasmar and Comtan. And the various drugs come in convenient pill sizes that are calibrated to give you the desired strength of medication.

Your neurologist has a medicine chest full of answers that can help you live a better quality of life. Therein lies *hope*. And *hope* keeps getting more promising and more promising as new treatments arrive on the scene. When first diagnosed, you are bound to be confused about what drug does what, why some people have multiple prescriptions, and what are the effects of each.

A lot depends upon the willingness of your physician to communicate. My introductory experience was not a good one. And after talking to a hundred or more Parkinson's People, it appears that my case was fairly well representative of the norm.

MY EXPERIENCE

My diagnosis went something like this: I walked the hall while the neurologist observed my gait and how I turned around. The doctor manipulated my limbs, then pinged me with a rubber-headed hammer. I wrote "Seattle is a rainy city" on a piece of paper and the doctor looked at it without expression. Then he announced, "We need an MRI on you. It's either a brain tumor or something else." I was so struck by the words "brain tumor" I never gave the "something else" a second thought.

After spending time in the MRI "Tunnel of Love," I talked the MRI technician into telling me what she saw. She said, "No sign of a brain tumor." I was relieved. Two weeks later I met with the neurologist. He spent two minutes with me and announced, "You have Parkinson's," The doctor handed me a prescription and told me to take the Eldepryl pills three times a day, then see him six months later.

I had an introduction to an unwanted problem that was not very comprehensive. "Take three pills a day and see me in six months" left me with some deep holes in knowledge about the disease and the function of certain medications. I had an excellent technician who was very professional in his diagnosis. He lacked the insight into the importance of putting me at ease about what I could expect from the medication. Fortunately, the Eldepryl had an immediate positive effect on my condition, and the dosage was the right amount. I didn't have any side effects, and had improvement in rigidity, the movement of my right arm, and my slowness changed for the better. This is not always the case for newly diagnosed Parkinson's People. You must work with your specialist to achieve the right medication, the right dosage, and the right scheduling of your dosage.

WHAT ABOUT NO MEDICATION

Before we get too deeply into pills and their role in the *hope* equation, let's consider the option of no medication. Often a newly diagnosed Parkinson's Person will be opposed to taking drugs. They decide to take the natural course. I know of several Parkinson's People who believe chemical substances are wrong for their body. They have held off for several years before seeking a neurologist's advice and prescriptions for various drugs. In one case, the tremor grew so severe that the person couldn't hold a fork still and would wildly beat his plate while trying to spear a piece of meat. He finally sought a neurologist for assistance. She prescribed medication and the pills worked wonders almost instantaneously. Now he eats a pleasurable meal without fear of stabbing his fellow diners. Before medication, there was little *hope* in this gentleman's life.

I know of another person who delayed medication until he was so depressed that he was ineffective in his job. He constantly dwelled on his worsening condition, yet he clung to the idea that aspirin was the only medication that he would ever take. He was a basket case. His friends convinced him to see a well-known neurologist. The doctor prescribed an agonist, and the Parkinson's symptoms immediately improved. So did his attitude. As well as *hope.*

It is admirable to be self-sufficient. But going without

medication is folly with this disease. Medication is the cornerstone to living a better quality of life. Just as it would be risky to let high blood pressure go untreated by medication, it would be equally foolish to not have medication assistance for Parkinson's.

SOME THOUGHTS ABOUT MEDICATION

It is not the purpose of this handbook to discuss in detail the various Parkinson's drugs. A good source of information on various medications and their purpose is a booklet available from the National Parkinson's Foundation. It is simply titled: "*Medications. Complete Guide for Parkinson's Patients.*" But the best information will come from your personal Parkinson's physician.

THE AIRPLANE ANALOGY

I've found that all of the Parkinson's drugs that have been prescribed by my physician are effective for a short period— usually about four hours. Then I must medicate again. It's like flying an airplane with a four-hour supply of fuel. A full gas tank will take you only so far. Then you must add more fuel or you'll crash and burn. Just as you shouldn't run the airplane down to the last gallon of gas in the tank, you shouldn't run your neurotransmitter system down to a marginal dopamine supply. Fine tuning the gas mixture is important to flying. Knowing how to balance your medication is just as critical to a dopamine-depleted brain. The only difference between the airplane and the Parkinson's Person is that you don't get to rest in the hangar. You have to keep fueling the dopamine tank, and fine tuning, day in and day out.

KEEPING A RECORD

Just as the airplane pilot keeps a log, you should keep a record of your physical performance and your chemical intake. This is particularly important if you're just getting started on a new medication or changing dosage. Notes on the positive or negative reactions, together with a precise record of the times you take the medication, will help you and your neurologist determine how to meter the most effective dosage to your neuro system. For example: Carl's physician recommended the following medication:

> One Sinemet 25/100 at 7 a.m.
> One Sinemet 25/100 at 11 a.m.
> One Sinemet 25/100 at 4 p.m.

Carl kept a record of precisely when he took the pills for a period of two weeks. He also noted the effects of the medication. He found that by 3 p.m. each day he became tired, slower and could hardly climb stairs. This was a red flag. Maybe the dosage period was too long between 11 a.m. and 4 p.m. He called his physician and reported his condition. Because Carl kept an accurate accounting over a two-week period, his physician was able to give a better analysis of the situation and alter the afternoon dosage. It may seem like a lot of detail work to keep track of your medication reaction 24 hours a day, but until you and your physician figure out the right balance it's essential that you do so.

IT'S A TEAM EFFORT

Remember: you and your physician are co-pilots—both of you are critical to the success of how well you maneuver through the Parkinson's flight plan. Your physician cannot solve your problem alone. He or she needs your input and cooperation. It requires a team effort. You have a first-hand knowledge of what's happening to your body and are obligated to accurately translate that to your physician. Without your input, the physician is asked to fly blindfolded.

STAY ON SCHEDULE

Be religious about taking the prescribed amount of your medication at exactly the same time of day–day in and day out.

Don't forget. Remember the airplane analogy. You don't want to run out of fuel. And if you happen to forget, don't double up on the medication when you remember several hours later. You'll throw the fine tuning of your neuro engine out of whack. In other words, don't try and overload your dopamine tank. It may cause some difficult-to-correct symptoms. Some Parkinson's People have wrist watches that are set to ping at appointed times throughout the day, as gentle reminders of "pill time." Others have pill boxes that they carry at all times. I have a little glass bottle that is about one-half inch in diameter and one inch long that conveniently fits in any pocket. I fill it each morning with my daily medication and force myself to remember to take it with me everywhere I go. Occasionally I have forgotten and paid the penalty of the full effects of Parkinson's.

Accept the idea that you'll probably be on medication for the remainder of your life. At first, that was a tough pill for me to swallow. But now it's such a part of me that I don't give it a second thought. I don't like the psychological tag of medication treatment, but I know without the little pills I would be a slower, less mobile, more rigid, and less involved person.

It may seem strange to have pills as a sign of *hope*. But there is such positive evidence that medication can improve the quality of life of Parkinson's People. Often it's not an easy task to find the right chemical combination. However, the odds are in your favor that you and your physician can work out a medication formula that will be a good solution to the unique symptoms that you must face daily. Hundreds of thousands of Parkinson's People are taking a similar dosage that you may be taking, and they are living quality lives. And therein lies *hope.*

WHAT YOU NEED IN A PHYSICIAN

Your physician is a critical person in your life if you are to experience *hope.* You may not have had a close relationship with a physician in the past. If you're like most people in the U.S., you have seen a doctor for a check up every five years or so, or only when you had a physical problem that was treated by a doctor you knew little about. If you've had an operation, the surgeon was no doubt in and out of the operating room without so much as a hand shake. You may have seen a specialist for one problem and another specialist for another ailment. The result has been you haven't been quite sure who was ultimately responsible for your well-being. There should be none of this with Parkinson's. You need a professional ally who is committed to building a long-term relationship. The attributes of your physician partner should be as follows:

1. A listener. Someone you know will hear your concerns and guide you to solutions. Someone who is

willing to take your phone call when "things aren't going quite right," and won't always pass you off to a nurse, or delay returning your call for three days.

2. <u>An active person.</u> Someone who is positive and firm about what you need to do. Someone who is up-to-date on the latest Parkinson's drugs and treatments. Someone in whom you have confidence.

3. <u>A empathetic person.</u> Someone who understands your condition. Someone who can identify with your tremor problem, your slowness, the occasions when you fumble with your wallet, and your constant fight to live a full life.

4. <u>An optimistic person.</u> Someone who believes Parkinson's is not a one-way ticket to early old age. Someone who gives you encouragement and makes your visits to his or her office a pleasant experience.

These are not unreasonable requests. You're on a pathway to *hope*. If you have a physician with a Dr. Droll disposition, it can't help but influence your attitude. That means you may have to change physicians several times or more before you find just the right match. Some medical plans are restrictive as to physician selection, and you may have to take the doctor the plan accepts. But if you have the opportunity to pick the best Parkinson's specialist in your community, do so. Don't be hesitant about moving from one doctor to another. Too often people are shy about telling a doctor they are changing to someone else because "I don't what to hurt her feelings." Nonsense. Doctors are used to patient changes. And most doctors accept the idea that no one physician is a good match for all Parkinson's People.

YOUR RESPONSIBILITIES

Your treatment is not a one-way street. Just as your physician has obligations to you, you have some clearly defined responsibilities to him or her. They run like this:

1. You must define your <u>current</u> problems clearly. It is most helpful for the doctor if you prepare a writen statement listing the three or four problems that you need answers to during your visit. Keep the list short and be specific. An example is:

Report to Dr. Smith
From Sally Hitchcock
October 21, 2001

<u>Problem No. 1</u>
I have nights in which I awaken five or six times. Sometimes I will lie awake for 30 to 40 minutes.

My last medication in the day is at 5 p.m. I retire around 10:30 p.m. How do we fix this?

Problem No. 2

Some days I can barely use my right hand. I have difficulty cutting meat or spearing salad. Often I will have to use my left hand while eating. This usually occurs during the evening meal. What can be done to improve my dexterity?

Problem No. 3

I get a freeze-up of my mouth so that my lips don't move to form words properly. This usually occurs around 9 a.m. after my 7 a.m. dosage. It seems to be related to the medication. Am I overdosing? If so, what can be done about it?

Record your physician's recommendations and keep them on file so you can refer to them periodically. Changes in your medication should be carefully monitored. A history of your scheduled medication will be most helpful. In other words, you must do your part to record your progress and not rely solely on the doctor to keep a file on you.

2. Don't treat your doctor's advice lightly. Follow his or her suggestions to the letter. This is particularly true with changes in medication dosage amounts and scheduling. You'll need a defined schedule if you are to have success with controlling the symptoms. If your doctor has used medical jargon you don't under stand, ask for a clarification. You shouldn't be confused when you leave the office. Ask for a written state- ment from the doctor regarding the medication schedule.

3. Be honest with your doctor. If you slip up with medication, 'fess up. If you're depressed at times, be open about it. The doctor is less effective if he or she can't see the whole you.

4. Use the phone judiciously. There will be times when you need to talk to your doctor right away. You feel you need help immediately. For example, you have had nausea for several days due to the medication you've been taking. You're at your wit's end. Call. Your doctor may be able to help you on the phone or may ask to see you in the office. But if you're simply wondering if you should take vitamin E along with your medication, save that question for

your next appointment. Be respectful of your doctor's time, and he or she will be more committed to helping you live a better quality of life.

5. Don't overstay your welcome. Your physician is a busy person. He is concerned about you. But he's also concerned about 100 or so other people. You want his undivided attention for your scheduled appointment but you should honor the 20 to 30 minutes that have been allocated just for you. This emphasizes the importance of being organized and to-the-point with your questions and about your state of health during your visit.

6. If you need support in expressing your concerns, have your spouse, caregiver, or significant other go to the appointment with you. Most movement disorder specialists welcome another person in the conversation. It may give new insight or perspective to the doctor.

7. Be sure to have a clear idea of when your next appointment will be. It may not be for three months but confirm with the doctor that you can call or see him or her before the scheduled time if you have complications.

Your physician can provide hope. He or she is the professional link to medication and professional advice that can make your life more enjoyable.

Now it's time to turn to the final letter of *hope*.

h·o·p·e·

IS

FOR

EXERCISE

Exercise can work wonders for Parkinson's People. It's absolutely essential that you take part in a daily routine of physical activity. Some days my body is much like the Tin Man in *The Wizard of Oz*. I clank around with rigid, stiff motions. Sometimes I find myself stooping forward when I walk, which throws my alignment off center, causing me to shuffle to regain balance. Often when I walk my right arm doesn't swing, which causes me to look like I've suffered a stroke on my right side. My Tin Man body needs lubrication and rehabilitation. Constantly. Not just one or two days a week. But every day. Exercise has been a miracle worker for me, and it can be for anyone in the early stages of the disease. The expression, "Use it or lose it" was never more true than with the Parkinson's crowd.

The degree of exertion should be approved by your physician. You don't want to injure yourself and then become so discouraged that you peter out entirely from any routine. Your physician should be able to determine the amount of exercise that's right for your condition without adverse consequences.

RUNNING

I have been a runner for 40 years. I ran a marathon when I was 52 years old. At 60 I could run eight-minute miles and usually ran three to five miles a day. I was diagnosed with Parkinson's when I was 66. Now, on a good day, I'll be fortunate to jog 13-to-14 minute miles over a two-mile stretch. Some days I can't run more than one mile without having to walk. My legs run out of gas due to Parkinson's. It's harder than the pre-Parkinson's days, but I view my slow, plodding ability to still maneuver around the neighborhood as a sign of *hope*. Particularly after I finish three miles of steadily putting one foot in front of another. I feel so alive. So healthy. So in tune with life.

I take along a Sony portable cassette player and listen to books on tape. There's nothing like hearing Jack London's White Fang while running on the sidewalk and being barked at by the neighbor's dog. It makes you step a little smarter and it does make you lengthen your stride.

BIKING

I alternate running with riding my bicycle for one hour-periods. As long as I can balance and pedal, I'll keep covering the area. There are about five different routes that I have mapped out. When I'm feeling good, I will tackle the hilly course. When I feel the dopamine isn't working up to par, I select the more level course. The biking gives variety to my exercise. If you're interested in biking, I recommend that you visit a local bike shop. Tell the bike shop owner you have Parkinson's, and ask for a suggestion as to the type of bike that will give you the most stability. I don't have a racing, skinny tires bike, and I don't have toe clips either. I'm in it for the pleasure and exercise value. You can't be in competition with the world if you have Parkinson's. You have to learn to maintain your own comfortable pace and not be bothered by the faster society. Hundreds of bikers passed me in the Seattle to Portland ride, but my objective wasn't to beat anybody. It was to complete the 200-mile distance.

Start out riding short distances on a route that is not loaded with fast-moving cars and trucks. There are lots of bicycle trails in cities all across the country. Here you'll find the ride is safer and less threatening. Later you can hit the roads when you feel more at ease on the bike.

THE BENEFITS

I don't advocate running for everyone, or cycling either. You don't have to be a sports-crazed individual to benefit from an exercise program. But I do believe everyone should find a physical activity that they can live with on a regular basis. Exercise will accomplish the following:

1. Keep your muscles and joints loose and able to move in a normal range of motion.

2. Keep your heart healthy and your circulation more normal.
3. Keep your lungs aerated and working to capacity.
4. Keep your mind stimulated and active.
5. Keep your kidneys and bladder working more efficiently.

How's that for five good reasons for *hope*? And as a special bonus, you'll find that your self-esteem will reach new heights. You'll feel more energetic, less tired, and willing to take on new risks. You should plan three days a week for exercise that works up sweat, gets the heart rate up and fills the lungs with air. And you should be committed to this program for the rest of your life—or until your body can't take it anymore or your doctor says stop. Too much to ask of someone who hasn't exercised in years? Not when you consider the probable downside of no effort—greater stiffness, less mobility and chances of Parkinson's influencing the negative outlook on your future.

MAKE IT EASY TO DO

Sue joined a health club when she was first diagnosed. She was determined to run the treadmill every day for 45 minutes and to follow up with the weight stations. This worked well

for a week. Then she found she was skipping workouts. It was just too much trouble to drive to the health club and often the machines were busy with other members. She changed her routine to 30 minute runs from her home at 7 a.m. three times a week, and 45 minute rides on her 21-speed bike on the weekends. It was more convenient operating from her home. You'll want to make your workout convenient to fit into your weekly schedule.

Whatever you decide to do aerobically—stationary biking, road biking, running, walking, step aerobics, swimming, cross country skiing or treadmill—make sure you set realistic goals for yourself. If you haven't been exercising on a regular basis, ease into the program. Don't try walking five miles the first day out. Exercise should be a pleasant experience—one you look forward to. It's the beginning of an integral part of your life for years to come. It has to become as regular a portion of your daily activities as eating lunch or going to bed each night.

Bill found that if he worked out at the same time every day it allowed him to schedule his life so that he didn't miss his vigorous walk every morning at 6 a.m.. If you exercise when you think you can "fit it in," chances are you won't do the fitting. Your body may not be firing on all cylinders in the early morning hours. In that case, find a time when you feel better about exercising. Once you commit to that time of the day, make sure you keep your appointment. Early morning seems best for me because I feel the freshness of a new day, people I encounter have a friendly "Good morning," the birds are happy, and it clears my mind for what I must undertake in the hours ahead.

Outdoor exercise is invigorating for me. But there are hundreds of Parkinson's People who commit to a workout on the stationary bike or treadmill in the privacy of their own home. I know of one woman who watches her favorite TV programs for an hour while she runs on her treadmill. She burns as many calories as someone in the street, and—for her—time seems to go faster with the TV viewing.

WORK INTO IT GRADUALLY

If your lifestyle has been more sedentary, it may be more difficult to suddenly don a pair of Nikes and start pumping your arms and legs. Here's a suggestion: try walking the neighborhood with your spouse or a friend at precisely the same time three times a week. Start out with going a half mile comfortably each outing the first week. Gradually work up to one mile. Then two miles. Then three. And who knows, you may turn into a power walker, ready for the next 10K in the city. The point is, no matter how non-athletic you have been in the past, you absolutely <u>must</u> undertake an exercise program if you have Parkinson's. This is not like a New Year's resolution.

It's a New Life's resolution.

SWEAT IS GOOD

The object is to get your heart pumping faster. Your muscles will need more oxygen as they work. Your heart will send extra oxygen through the blood stream to your muscles. This increased activity of your heart makes this vital organ grow stronger. And the entire circulatory system is rejuvenated because blood flow is distributed evenly to all the blood vessels. It's like revving up the engine in your car and giving it a good test drive three times a week. That's surely better than keeping the car motionless and on idle all the time. For instance, while you are sitting eating potato chips and drinking a Coke, your heart pumps about six quarts of blood a minute. But when an adult male exercises vigorously, the heart pumps about 25 quarts of blood a minute throughout the body.

STRETCHING IS VITAL

I exercise seven days a week. Physical therapists say three to four times a week is all you need. However, stretching <u>every day</u> should be an integral part of your exercise program. Parkinson's Disease can affect nearly every muscle in your body—your shoulders, your legs, your neck, your feet, even your facial expression. You're stiffer and less flexible. You're slower to react. You're probably not as agile as you used to be. And possibly your balance is not what it was before. If you don't limber up your body every day, it will become just like the Tin Man's. With five to ten minutes of devoted stretching each and every day, there's *hope* for a more flexible body.

There are a number of good books and handbooks on specific stretching exercises for Parkinson's People. Write The National Parkinson's Association or American Parkinson's Disease Association. Or get hold of the best stretching book for athletes: *Stretching* by Bob Anderson, illustrated by Jean Anderson. To me, this is the Bible of the health and fitness field. The illustrations are outstanding and the chapters are divided to cover every part of your body. Plus, there are recommended stretching exercises for nearly every sport you can name.

CHECK WITH A PT

It would probably be a good idea to have an appointment with a physical therapist before you begin your exercise activity. Choose someone who is familiar with your disease. They will be able to map out a program that will fit your capacity and interests. They can become another segment in your *hope* team—someone you can lean on when the going gets tough.

Tai Chi is highly recommended as an excellent therapy

for Parkinson's. You can find classes throughout your area. Also, there are videotapes on Tai Chi. People who take organized classes seem to do better with the personal attention they get than those who have to interpret the moves in front of a TV set. Classes at specific times get you organized as well. A physical therapist can suggest competent Tai Chi instructors.

SOME DAILY SUGGESTIONS

I've found four things that help my posture. One is putting my hands on my hips and thrusting my shoulders back. This hands-on-the-hips technique works wonders. You can do this while waiting in line at the bank. Fill your lungs with air and feel the difference in your body.

Number two also is a standing-in-line exercise. Try standing on one foot for 30 seconds or so. Rest your left foot behind your right calf and concentrate your eyes on a distant object. Then try standing on your right foot. You'll probably find you have better balance on one side than the other.

Number three is a good morning and just-before-bed stretch. Bring your arms fully extended over your head with your arms as close to your ears as possible. Keep your chin up. Stretch to try to touch the ceiling and hold for ten seconds. Repeat four or five times.

Number four can be conducted each day after your

shower or bath. Stretch your bath towel behind your shoulder blades, grasp the towel at its ends and stretch the towel as tight as possible, forcing the shoulders back and the chest out. Repeat this three times, holding it for 30 seconds. Then bring the hands closer together on the towel, and force the shoulders back and chest out. Repeat this three times and hold for 30 seconds.

A WORD ABOUT WATER

Drink water. And plenty of it. Parkinson's People often have difficulty swallowing, so their tendency is to take little sips. You may think you're consuming lots of liquid, but it takes a lot of sipping to meet the requirements of an active, exercising body. You need to take in two quarts of water a day. That's eight glasses of eight ounces. I've found that a sports water bottle is a handy way to measure the water I drink but I don't manage to swallow as well out of the narrow opening. Other Parkinson's People tell me the same thing. Therefore, I fill an eight-ounce glass of water and keep it by the kitchen sink. I drink and refill the glass throughout the day. If I'm away from home, I usually carry a water bottle, but the kitchen sink reminder is the best solution for my Parkinson's needs.

Most physical trainers recommend that you drink water before, during, and after exercise. You can become dehydrated faster than you may think. If your mouth is dry and you feel thirsty, your body is telling you that you are many minutes late in taking in water. It's a signal your water intake is out of balance.

You can tell if you are drinking enough fluids through-out the day by monitoring your urine. Urine that is dark yellow is a bad sign. It can mean dehydration. Urine that is clear in color probably means you are drinking adequate amounts of fluid. It's easy to forget. But so terribly important. Don't rely on coffee, soda, or tea to be your fluid supply. Count your water intake.

EXERCISING THE MIND

One part of your body that should not be overlooked is your mind. Keeping it sharp and healthy is also a vital part of maintaining hope for Parkinson's People. This requires a daily commitment to explore new information that will challenge the brain to be an integral activity of your everyday life. Otherwise, this magnificent organ may become a message-sender that repeatedly says: "I can't." "I'm not up to it." "It's beyond me" or "I used to, but not now." There is nothing worse than to see people who have let their brain-power grow stagnant. Don't get trapped into believing that because your body moves more slowly that your mind will be just as slow to grasp ideas. I've seen many Parkinson's People function in high-level decision making roles with keen insight into handling complicated problems.

This is one area that I have found to provide the greatest encouragement in living with the disease—so far it has not changed my ability to reason and assimilate new thoughts. But I do try to work my mind as hard as I pedal my bike. And I do it constantly. I liken it to stretching a hamstring or a back muscle. Stretching the mind is critical to overall health of your body.

Here are five ways that have helped keep my mind stretched and have resulted in a healthier mental outcome since I've been diagnosed with Parkinson's:

1. <u>Chess.</u> The strategies in this game are a real mind expander. I bought a book for beginners and am learning the basic moves. The only opponents I have beaten are my 8 year old and 10 year old grandchildren. But who knows, someday I may be up against a Russian champion. You've got to believe.

2. <u>Crossword puzzles</u>. I've found you don't have to start with the New York Times edition. I was not a "puzzle nut" prior to Parkinson's. I started with a simple puzzle book that I purchased at a newsstand. The exercise keeps my mind oiled and ready to accept new twists of thought in verbal problem solving. There is no greater delight than getting

100% right on the daily drill.

3. <u>Research project.</u> I became fascinated with the Children's Crusade which took place in the year 1212. Researching this period has opened a new world of history with which I was unfamiliar. What I will do with the information I am uncertain but my mind is running on all cylinders. You no doubt have "things" you wonder about. The book store, library and internet are begging you to uncover new information.

4. <u>College class.</u> I audited a class at the University of Washington on "The European Economy." It was composed of 80 students and an excellent professor who got my brain juices flowing at a new level. In exploring the classes available, I was inspired to expand my mind in directions I hadn't considered in years. Courses in philosophy, Chinese history, religions of the world, psychology and leaders of the 20th century all tantalize my brain cells.

5. <u>The computer.</u> I was uneasy about changing over from a Mac to a PC. I bit the bullet, mostly with my wife's encouragement, and wound up in a "Word" class at the nearby community college. I found that some of the younger people were just as new to the PC world as I was. Now my mind

works fairly well with my new Dell and I don't panic when the little paper clip man gives me a disgusted look of scorn.

These examples are not expressed as absolute guidelines. They are merely examples of how one person works to keep the mind active. You may hate crossword puzzles. But chances are if you set your mind to it, you can come up with ideas that do interest you. Maybe it's cooking and following complicated recipes. Or Civil War history. Or genealogy. Or bridge. Or cribbage. Or managing the family finances.

The important thing to remember is: *keeping the mind exercised is just as important to your overall health as the sweat you work up doing repetitions in the gym.* A stimulated mind is a mind full of hope.

GIVE YOURSELF A BREAK

Rest days are necessary for athletes in training in order to keep from burning out or causing injury. You, too, will find that a breather from time to time will revitalize your exercise endeavors, keep you fresh, and stimulate renewal of your commitment to physical fitness. If you're flirting with "feeling sorry for yourself" it's perfectly natural and OK. Take time out to digest what's going on in your mind and body. Give yourself a fixed time to be negative. Say 30 minutes. Add up what's going right and what's going wrong. If you can't get back on track after that period of time you may be more seriously depressed than you thought. Then you need to see your doctor. Fortunately, depression is treatable. So there's *hope* there as well.

IT'S UP TO YOU

I wish I could say it's going to be fun and easy. I <u>can</u> say you're going to look and feel better. But there will be days when you don't want to face the rain and wind. Or watching Good Morning, America as you pedal that stationary bike just doesn't have it some mornings. But there's no shortcut if you are committed to the road to a better quality of life. Your body will love you for it. And I'll bet you'll get comments from friends who say, "George, you sure look good." or "Betty, you're doing so well. I'd never know you have Parkinson's."

The other option is doing nothing. The results are predictable here as well. You'll continue to get stiffer. You'll probably be more bent over when you walk. Chances are you'll shuffle more. You could have more falls caused by lack of strength and balance. You could be discouraged and more depressed. In other words, you'll be playing right into the hands of the disease.

I know of Parkinson's People who are still skiing at 75, shooting 80's in golf, climbing 8,000-foot mountains, and sailing rough waters. They have *hope*. And you can too.

THE FOUR KEY WORDS TO HOPE

There you have it. HELP. OPTIMISM. PHYSICIAN. EXERCISE. They add up to **HOPE**.

Parkinson's is such a part of me that the inconveniences of the disease seem natural. As though I were selected for some strange reason to awaken each day for the rest of my life with the reality that my body has dramatically changed. I can't correct that. But I can accept it. I can share my experiences with those who care to listen. And maybe, just maybe, the road I've followed can help smooth the transition of those who have recently been diagnosed with Parkinson's. If this changes the life and gives *hope* to just one person who has Parkinson's, then I will consider this endeavor worthwhile.